ERSHIRE BEACON LOOKING SOUTH

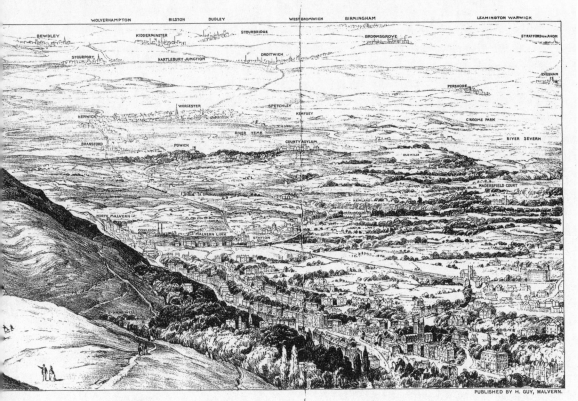

STERSHIRE BEACON LOOKING NORTH

Bygone
MALVERN

THE SHALLOW BATH.

" Your true life preserver."

Bygone
MALVERN

Pamela Hurle

Phillimore

1989

Published by
PHILLIMORE & CO. LTD.,
Shopwyke Hall, Chichester, Sussex

ISBN 0 85033 725 9

Printed and bound in Great Britain by
BIDDLES LTD.,
Guildford, Surrey

Contents

List of Illustrations

Introduction and Acknowledgements

The pleasant Worcestershire town of Malvern, nestling against the Malvern Hills, is home to about thirty thousand people, but a haven for many thousands more, seeking recreation in a part of the country where natural scenery and beautiful views refresh minds and bodies in need of a holiday. Malvern has been such a retreat since Victorian times: when the 18-year-old Victoria came to the throne in 1837 Malvern was a little village on the brink of being transformed into a flourishing spa town.

The purpose of this book is to provide glimpses of Malvern in the past, using contemporary material not now widely available. Some readers may see it as a useful companion to *Portrait of Malvern*; it is, however, in itself a perspective picture of those features of Malvern's development which have contributed to today's town.

Many of us have a tendency to view the past through romantic eyes. This usually harmless foolishness might be encouraged by some of the extracts from early guide-books and histories, and by idealised views, but I hope that the comments which follow will paint a more realistic picture than that created by the literary, artistic – or was it commercial? – licence of the original authors and artists. A dip into the nostalgic past is very pleasant, but a healthy scepticism as we peek under the attractive wrapping will probably leave us thankfully aware of the blessings of the end of the 20th century.

I am most grateful for the loan of material owned by people who share an interest in preserving something of Malvern's past. Loans from Humphrey Bartleet, Dennis Firkins, John Guise, June Hebden, Brian Iles, Margaret Jago, Myrtle and Donald Pembridge, Richard Powell, Kenneth Rickards, Hubert Squibb, Dr. R. Alan Sutton and the Welsh Industrial and Maritime Museum have added immensely to any interest that this book may generate. The mammoth task of reproducing this material was undertaken by Jerry Mullaney, whose care and interest have ensured not only the highest possible standard of pictures, but, equally important, the safe return of all that was loaned. To all of these kind people I express my very sincere thanks.

Of course, none of this would have been possible without the work of writers, artists and photographers who are long since dead. Where possible, I have acknowledged their work. Many must remain anonymous but it is these authors and illustrators who really made this book possible: they – often unwittingly – are the means by which we may still obtain glimpses of a way of life which has now gone for ever. We all owe a great debt to these unknown preservers of our heritage.

As always, I have a special thank you to my husband without whose encouragement I would not have published a single book. This time he has also initiated me into the mysteries of the word processor, thus manifesting not only the skills of the scientist but the patience of Job.

PAMELA HURLE

April 1989

xii

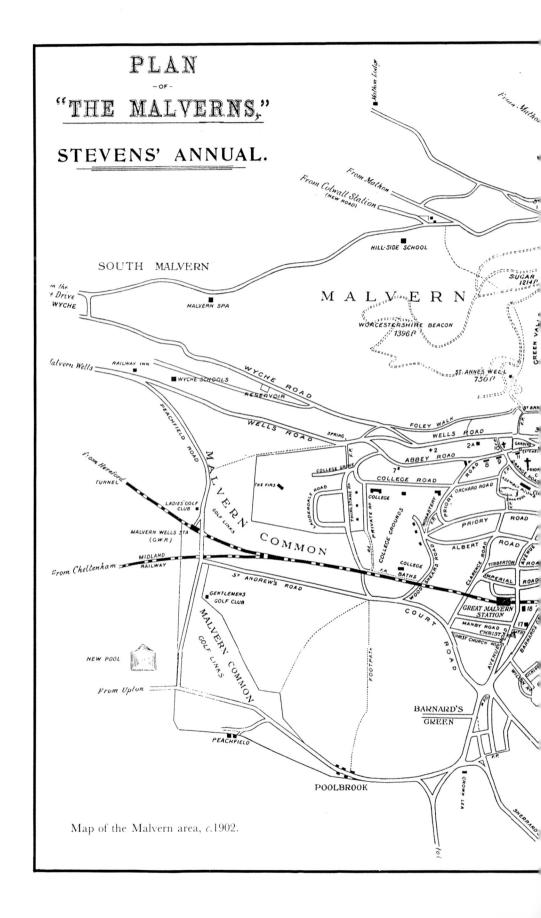

Map of the Malvern area, *c.*1902.

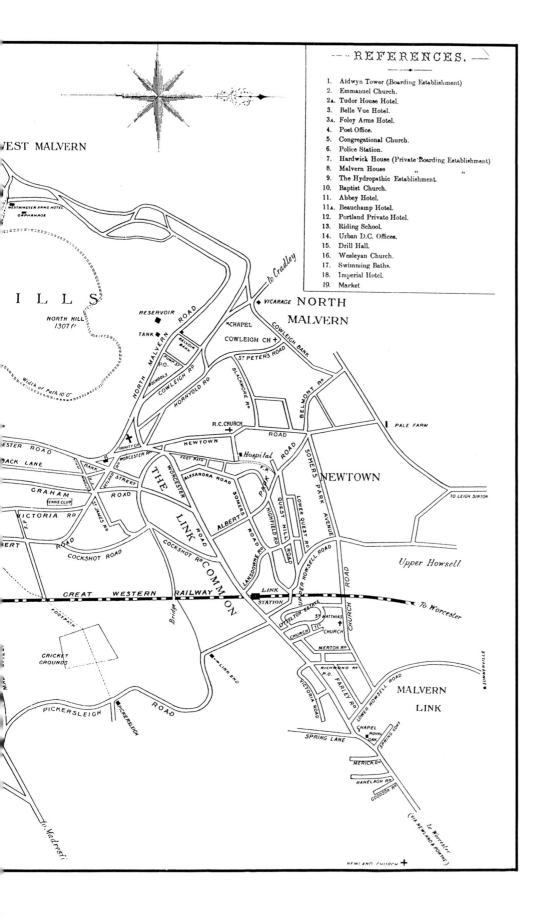

Chapter One

The Evolution of Malvern

Before dipping into those sources which tell us about a Malvern that is largely lost, it would be as well to have some clear outline of the features which have contributed to making Malvern the unusual and attractive town that we know today.

Above all else, the landscape is significant, both nature and man having left indelible marks upon it. The Malvern Hills, rising dramatically from the plain, were surrounded in pre-historic and medieval times by thousands of acres of wilderness, virtually untouched by man for centuries. Two Iron-Age forts on Midsummer Hill and the Herefordshire Beacon were the result of a massive community effort to provide accommodation for several thousand settlers over a period of four or five hundred years but these people disappeared with the arrival of Roman forces in the first century A.D. Their dispersal at this time is now believed to have been coincidental, but it was long thought that the British chieftain, Caractacus, resisted the Romans from the Malverns. This belief led Worcestershire's great musician, Sir Edward Elgar, to entitle one of his most famous works *Caractacus*: Elgar, having spent much of his life in the Malvern area, was steeped in its history and legend. The courage of Caractacus forms one of our national legends but there is no satisfactory evidence for the assumption that the Malverns provided the battleground, despite the efforts, in 1822, of Dr. Card, the vicar of Malvern, to claim this distinction in his pretentious and not very readable dissertation.

A few Roman finds indicate that the Romans passed this way and may have had small settlements in the Leigh Sinton and Malvern Link areas. In any event, Britain was on the fringes of their empire and Worcestershire was of no great importance to them so their impact here was slight. Much more lasting was the influence of the first Norman king, 1,000 years later: William the Conqueror designated thousands of acres in Worcestershire, Herefordshire and Gloucestershire as royal forest, in which special laws protected the deer and their environment – the 'venison and the vert' – to provide sport for kings and nobles. These laws left a permanent mark on the landscape because they specifically forbade the felling of trees or clearance of forest without a licence, thus ensuring that for centuries a vast tract remained largely undeveloped. When the forest laws were rescinded in the 17th century new farms were carved out of the virgin wasteland, but a large acreage of wasteland was preserved and, when encroachment and enclosure threatened it in the 19th century, local people ensured its retention by setting up the body that still safeguards over 3,000 acres of hill and common land – the Malvern Hills Conservators.

The Norman period also saw the establishment of small priories at Great Malvern and at Little Malvern. Although, like all monasteries, they were dissolved by Henry VIII, the monks' churches are still used for worship. At Little Malvern a mere fragment of the priory church remains; at Great Malvern the mid-16th-century purchase of the church which the monks had enlarged and embellished only 50 years earlier has given the parish the distinction of having today one of the largest and most beautiful parish churches in England. When the parishioners scratched together the few pounds

1. This picture of British Camp, or the Herefordshire Beacon, appeared in John Chambers' *History of Malvern*, published in 1817. It clearly shows the ramparts which are still visible on the hill. For over 400 years the site was occupied by ancient Britons from the Dobunni tribe.

needed for the purchase, their most immediate concern was to avoid, by taking over the monks' church, having to restore their ancient dilapidated parish church, dedicated to St Thomas, which stood at the top of Church Street. The priory church, thus snatched from the hands of the demolition workers in the 16th century, nearly collapsed from neglect 250 years later but was saved again in the nick of time. With the old gatehouse which once commanded the entrance into the monastic estate, it still stands as a reminder of our medieval roots, providing tangible evidence of how religion permeated society and ecclesiastical buildings were focal points.

The loss of the priories in the 16th century and of the forest in the 17th meant that Malvern had no features to distinguish it from a host of other small villages except that on its hills were several springs of water reputed to have unusual qualities. In the mid-18th century Dr. John Wall's analysis at last pinpointed what made Malvern water so special – it contained very few minerals and was exceptionally pure:

The Malvern water, says Dr. John Wall,
Is famed for containing just nothing at all.

This gift of nature was not fully exploited until the mid-19th century when Dr. Wilson and Dr. Gully set up hydropathic establishments in the village, turning it within 20 years into a thriving town which annually attracted thousands of visitors, many of them quite affluent.

The strict régime of the water-cure doctors – plenty of exercise, fresh air, plain food and Malvern water – worked wonders on the overfed and often alcohol-soaked bodies of those who could afford their fees. Not until the end of the century did scepticism –

2. This print by J. Bradley of the gateway to Malvern's medieval priory is one of many romanticised portrayals of the building. The print pre-dates the extensive restoration of the gateway in the late 19th century.

3. When Wood produced this print Malvern was still a sleepy village and its sparse population was only beginning to realise the need to restore and protect its church on which the medieval monks had lavished so much work and money.

.A DRINK AT ST ANNE'S WELL.

THE SITZ BATH.
Hatching Health.

4. Examples of the many cartoons and sketches published during the 19th century. These reflect a wry humour about the water cure – and the money to be made from tempting visitors to buy pictures, walking-sticks and various knick-knacks.

THE SHALLOW BATH.
"Your true life preserver."

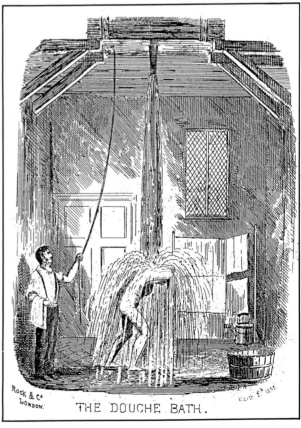

THE DOUCHE BATH.

5. Malvern College in its early days. The ivy has now been removed and at the top of the steps shown here St George now stands – the college's dignified memorial to its many former pupils who fell in war.

and a bout of typhoid – blight the fortunes of those who made their living out of patients and other visitors who saw hydropathy as a panacea for almost all ills.

By the early 20th century the water-cure was finished, and the Malvern Hills were threatened by quarriers who made profits from the growing demand for stone to build roads fit for use by motor vehicles. The town was once again a rather sleepy backwater though, admittedly, with a certain air of gentility. This was encouraged by the presence of several independent schools, notably Malvern College, a public school for boys founded in 1865, and Malvern Girls' College whose origins go back to 1893.

In an unexpected manner it was Malvern College which was to provide the opportunity for Malvern to adapt once more. In 1942 its buildings were requisitioned by the government: a suitable safe base was needed for work on radar and other scientific developments which were to play so decisive a role in the defeat of Hitler. Malvern people did not make the scientists welcome, possibly because their work made Malvern more vulnerable in the event of a Nazi onslaught, but in fact their presence ensured that Malvern has had a viable economy from 1942 until the present time.

This, then, in broad outline, is the story of Malvern. The rest of this book aims to give contemporary glimpses of Malvern as it has developed and changed during the last two centuries.

Chapter Two

Malvern in the Early 19th Century

This is the first period for which we have detailed knowledge of Malvern, and for this we are largely dependent on two sources: *A History of Malvern* by John Chambers (1817) and *A Description of Malvern* by Mary Southall (1822). Mrs. Southall was the wife of the priory church organist, John Southall, and, since they kept the Library (now Barclays Bank) in the centre of Malvern, her real purpose was presumably commercial, for her guide-book was one of many items sold there to both local residents and visitors. Her unashamed plagiarism of John Chambers' book indicates the limited scope of her own research but the two authors together give us, with both text and illustrations, a vivid picture of a Malvern not yet transformed by the doctors who came in the 1840s to exploit Malvern water.

It was, nevertheless, a Malvern beginning to feel the need for a pleasing public image.

Since 1740 the Foley family of Stoke Edith, a few miles away in Herefordshire, had been lords of the manor of Malvern and Edward Foley began, in 1819, to employ architects, builders and other craftsmen to modernise and beautify the approach to Malvern from Worcester. Samuel Deykes, an old and respected Malvern inhabitant, had started a small library, which was enlarged by John Southall. Edward Foley then thought it appropriate to erect a building 'suited to the rising importance of Great Malvern' and selected for its site

6. Stoke Edith House, destroyed by fire in the 20th century, was a brick and stone building completed in the first part of the 18th century. Set in a vast park, with 'noblest timber trees' and 'charming and highly picturesque views', it was much admired. Inside, great attention had been paid to detail and the grand staircase and entrance hall were painted with 'allegorical subjects by Sir James Thornhill'. (From Southall's *Description of Malvern*.)

that part of the village which most particularly required improvement . . . It must be confessed that much of an auxiliary nature upon the opposite side of the way, remains to be done, in order to display the building with suitable effect, and to render complete the improvement of what may be considered the entrance to Great Malvern.

This was a jibe at the smithy nearly opposite the recently extended *Foley Arms*.

7a.　The Library built in the early 19th century is now Barclays Bank. The Greeks being, as Mary Southall put it, 'a most civilized and learned people' the classical Greek style of architecture was chosen for the Library. Its reading room was well stocked with newspapers and periodicals while elsewhere in the building it was possible to buy perfume, stationery, snuff, patent medicines or even 'fine toned, grand, horizontal and small square Piano-Fortes'. These instruments could also be hired by the week or month.

RULES
OBSERVED BY THE COMPANY
at the
CONVERSAZIONE,
HELD ONCE A FORTNIGHT,
in the
PUBLIC-ROOM, LIBRARY HOUSE,
Malvern.

Each subscriber, for the season, pays ten shillings and sixpence, and one shilling and sixpence per night, for tea and coffee.

Each non-subscriber pays one shilling each night, admission, and one shilling and sixpence, for tea and coffee.

Each player pays one shilling and sixpence for cards, unless he choose to play with cards which have been played with before; the charge then is only ninepence.

The company meet every Monday fortnight, in their walking dresses, a full dress being against the rules, at seven o'clock in the evening, and break up at eleven. They amuse themselves with Reading, Conversation, Cards, Chess, Drafts, Backgammon, Bagatelle, or their work. If the company dance a Quadrille, previous notice must be given, so that a Harper or Violin player may be procured. To defray the expense, one shilling and sixpence is paid.

The design of the Conversazione, is to promote sociability, and to gain society for the visitors. The proprietor therefore solicits the patronage and support of the Ladies and Gentlemen residents of Malvern. It was proposed, page 10, that the Conversazione should take place once a week, which has been objected to, as too often.

7b.　The Conversazione referred to in this advertisement was held once a fortnight from 7 p.m. until 11 p.m.

7c.　The terms at Southall's Boarding-house included use of the impressive library and early 19th-century luxuries – tea and sugar.

THE FOLLOWING TERMS
OF
SOUTHALL'S BOARDING-HOUSE,
FOR A SELECT PARTY,
NOT EXCEEDING FOURTEEN PERSONS, WITH
THE RULES
to be observed, may serve to give the stranger some idea of the expences, and accommodations.

An elegant Drawing Room, at the south end of the House, feet by 14, (see plate of the Library, page 53.) is provided, for the general use of the Boarders; with the use of the Library, and Reading Room, for which no charge is made.

The company assemble and dine at the public table, in a handsome Dining Room, at half past four o'clock, each day. The first bell is rung at four and the dinner bell at half past four.

Every Lady and Gentleman is requested to settle with the master of the house, for board, lodging, &c. at the end of every week, commencing from the time of each person's arrival.

No petition from travelling beggars, suffered to be presented, or hung up in the rooms, without permission of the master of the house.

Any person engaging lodgings, must pay for them, from the day they are engaged.

All who board in the house, are free of expense at the Conversazione, music and cards excepted.

TERMS.	£.	s.	d.
Board, per Week, including Tea and Sugar, and the Use of the Library and Reading Room,	2	2	0
Bed Room, from 7s. to	1	1	0
Dining only,	1	4	0
A Gentleman introducing a Friend to Breakfast,	0	1	9
Ditto Lunch,	0	1	0
Ditto Dinner,	0	4	0
Ditto to Tea,	0	1	6
Ditto to Supper,	0	1	6
Lights, per Week,	0	1	6
Servant's Board, including Tea for Breakfast,	1	2	0
Afternoon Tea, for upper servants,	0	2	6
Man Servant's Bed,	0	2	6
Separate Rooms, for ditto,	0	7	0

8. This 19th-century photograph gives some idea of the buildings opposite the *Foley Arms*.

Later on in the 19th century, when Malvern had been graced with the presence of royal visitors, the Library became the Royal Library, forming a majestic endpiece to a row of impressive buildings financed by the lord of the manor, whose bills and accounts may be inspected at the Record Office in Hereford. Next to the Library were the Baths and Pump Room. Originally built in the early 1820s, the baths, including a 'cold plunging bath' were 'commodious and elegant'. Later, additional floors were built over the ground floor to accommodate the flourishing wine and spirit business started by Edward Archer in the 1830s. A little further along the road to Worcester the *Foley Arms*, or *Down's Hotel*, was built.

The object of early 19th-century building was to improve the main Worcester to Ledbury road, and included the setting out of Belle Vue Terrace as we know it today. It was Deykes, again, who

has suggested a new feature of elegant and comprehensive beauty, which, when executed, will combine essential advantages and conveniences to Malvern . . . The prettiest part of Malvern is perhaps the line above the church, where the Belle Vue Hotel is situated. It may almost be called a terrace. Proceeding thence, along the road to Hereford, there is a very considerable curve to the right, and the road afterwards assumes a convex form round the base of the hills. To return thence to Malvern, at this point, the Library may be seen, but is lost sight of, on continuing along the road. The suggestion is, to erect a rough parapet wall at certain given points, to fill up the chasm from the hills, level with the present road, by which a most enchanting line of straight and level carriage-drive would be made, directly into Malvern, and the curve in which the road now runs, might be

9. The *Foley Arms*, or *Downs' Hotel* was, according to Mary Southall, built in 1810 'from a plan drawn by Mr. Samuel Deykes' but its proprietor, Mr. Downs, soon had to add two wings. It retains its name to the present day though for a period in the 19th century rejoiced in the addition of *Royal Kent and Coburg* to its name. This reflected royal visitors to Malvern though the young Victoria and her mother the Duchess of Kent actually stayed nearby at Holly Mount rather than at the hotel. Victoria never came as queen to Malvern.

10. The Abbey House, which stood for many years on the south side of the Abbey Gateway, was demolished in the mid-19th century by William Archer. When he replaced it with The Abbey Hotel he also demolished what he saw as an unsightly barn. It was actually the ancient guesten hall of the priory, and many Malvernians – past and present – thought its loss an unforgivable act of vandalism.

11. To the left of the *Belle Vue Hotel* was the *Crown*. John Chambers referred to a meeting of the Friendly Society held at the *Crown* in Great Malvern in 1754, so Mary Southall may have been right in supposing it to have been the village's oldest hotel. It was also used – perhaps just a room or two – as a school kept by George Roberts in the 18th century. Mrs. Southall also claimed that under the ownership of Mr. Beard (see board at side) part of the *Belle Vue* was attached to the *Crown* and used 'as a coffee and subscription newspaper room. The house has undergone many alterations . . . It is now in the occupation of Mr. Harrison. From the gardens of this house you may ascend the hill to St Ann's Well.' It was also at the *Crown* that Dr. James Wilson started practising hydropathy in the three years before he built his own Priessnitz House (now Park View) in 1845.

> appropriated to villas or a crescent. The situation would be exquisite and, as a promenade and drive, it would be unequalled, both in respect to its altitude and command of scenery.

From this carefully laid out terrace one would look over the plot now called Belle Vue Island and see Church Street in which a few cottages stood in their gardens and orchards. Beyond these was the turnpike house at the junction of the road down to Barnard's Green with the lane (Priory Road) which led to the Chalybeate Spring. The steeply sloping top of Church Street, then known as Paradise Row, was occupied by lodging-houses, while opposite Belle Vue, on the site now occupied by the Post Office, was the vicarage, described in 1819 as wearing

> the appearance of a cottage ornée, its front is covered with jessamine, and it is almost invisible to the eye from the laurels and other evergreens planted near it. It is situate near the church. . .almost facing the Crown Hotel, whose stables, near the Abbey House, are a disgrace to this charming village.

On the right hand side of Church Street itself was the old priory church secluded by trees, tempting numerous artists to depict it in a romanticised manner that encouraged blissful ignorance of the leaking roof, flooded floors, decaying seats and 'lumber'. The ivy shown so picturesquely entwining itself around the windows was, in fact, threatening to cause the east end of the church to collapse.

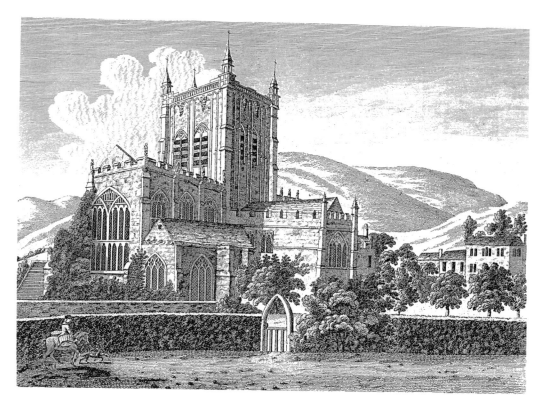

12. One of many rather stylised prints of Malvern Priory, this one dating from the late 18th century, shows the encroachment of the ivy which threatened the structure. The detail of the original picture also reveals in the north transept the pigeon loft which had caused great offence to a visitor in 1788. He had expressed comprehensive disapproval: of the condition of the church, of the habits of local schoolboys who amused themselves throwing stones at its medieval stained glass, and of the vicar who seemed negligent of his duty to safeguard the building. All his criticism seems perfectly justifiable!

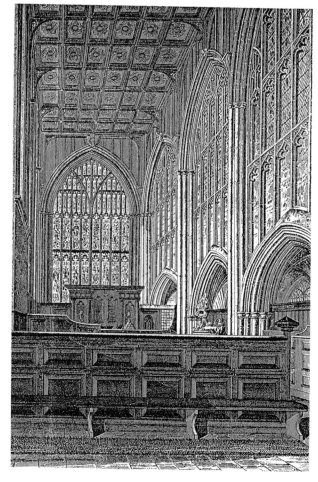

13. The interior of Great Malvern Priory Church in 1824.

About 1812 an appeal launched by the vicar, Dr. Richard Graves, enabled money to be spent, rather foolishly, in 'repairing and restoring the ceiling' and applying 'a most beautiful quantity of' whitewash:

> the venerable edifice became indeed a whitened sepulchre; for although neatness or, at least, cleanliness, reigned above, ruin and devastation bore sovereign sway below; confusion and dilapidation strove for mastery, and rubbish and dirt mocked all the plasterer's art to restore it to comfort.

At least the pigeon loft of Dr. Graves' predecessor seemed no longer to adorn the eastern wall of the Jesus Chapel but when Dr. Henry Card took over from Dr. Graves in 1815 the church was clearly in a most unfortunate condition. Card raised more money, commenting nearly 20 years later that

> Malvern Church indeed seems fated to experience every sort of spoliation. Its very porch has fallen into lay hands; and its roof would not now have been crumbling into ruins, had not the lead been stolen. Its exterior truly may be compared to those cabinets of ivory one sometimes meets with in old family mansions, scratched, flawed, splintered, carrying all the marks of time-worn decay.

In view of the concern expressed by Card about the state of the priory, it is sad that his own efforts to care for the church fell far short of what was required. When the architect Pugin came to Malvern in 1833 he castigated those who had carried out superficial repairs, saving his most scathing remarks for those who had put up a window with

14. Dr. Henry Card as a young man. His position as tutor to Edward Foley was doubtless a significant factor in his being appointed to the vicarage of Malvern in 1815, for Foley was patron of the living. Card stayed here until his death in 1844 but letters exchanged between him and his patron show that they did not always see eye to eye.

> the arms of the subscribers in stained glass, with their names in full, a monument of their folly and arrogance. The very mullions in which the glass is placed are rotten and falling. The church itself is in dreadful repair; fall it must and all that is to be hoped is, that in its fall it may annihilate those whose duty it was to restore it.

Malvern had numerous benefactors at this time, some of their names appearing, not pompously in the stained glass window, but in the features and places of interest to which Mrs. Southall referred in a fascinating sketch map of the hills with its accompanying key.

The Hon. Mr. Damer 'with his family were very great benefactors to this place, when in an infant state' and he provided the walk, with its strategically placed seats, leading from the Well House to Foley Terrace. General Buchanan's Walk connected Damer's Walk with Merrick's Walk at the Sugar Loaf: Buchanan 'to whom the inhabitants of Malvern are greatly indebted' also gave his name to that part of Church Street now occupied by Woolworth's and the National Westminster Bank.

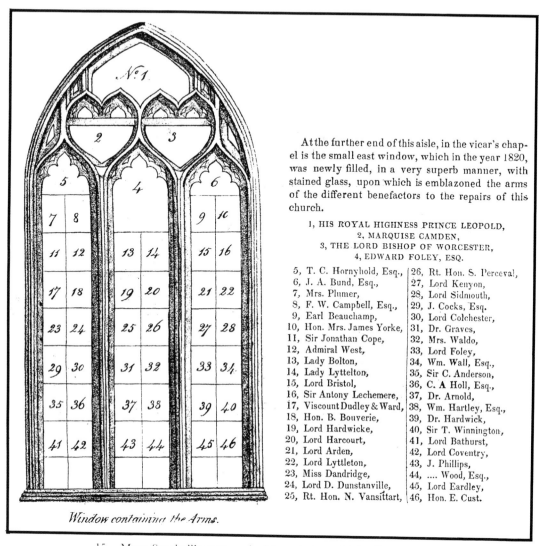

At the further end of this aisle, in the vicar's chapel is the small east window, which in the year 1820, was newly filled, in a very superb manner, with stained glass, upon which is emblazoned the arms of the different benefactors to the repairs of this church.

1, HIS ROYAL HIGHNESS PRINCE LEOPOLD,
2, MARQUISE CAMDEN,
3, THE LORD BISHOP OF WORCESTER,
4, EDWARD FOLEY, ESQ.

5, T. C. Hornyhold, Esq.,
6, J. A. Bund, Esq.,
7, Mrs. Plumer,
8, F. W. Campbell, Esq.,
9, Earl Beauchamp,
10, Hon. Mrs. James Yorke,
11, Sir Jonathan Cope,
12, Admiral West,
13, Lady Bolton,
14, Lady Lyttelton,
15, Lord Bristol,
16, Sir Antony Lechemere,
17, Viscount Dudley & Ward,
18, Hon. B. Bouverie,
19, Lord Hardwicke,
20, Lord Harcourt,
21, Lord Arden,
22, Lord Lyttleton,
23, Miss Dandridge,
24, Lord D. Dunstanville,
25, Rt. Hon. N. Vansittart,
26, Rt. Hon. S. Perceval,
27, Lord Kenyon,
28, Lord Sidmouth,
29, J. Cocks, Esq.
30, Lord Colchester,
31, Dr. Graves,
32, Mrs. Waldo,
33, Lord Foley,
34, Wm. Wall, Esq.,
35, Sir C. Anderson,
36, C. A Holl, Esq.,
37, Dr. Arnold,
38, Wm. Hartley, Esq.,
39, Dr. Hardwick,
40, Sir T. Winnington,
41, Lord Bathurst,
42, Lord Coventry,
43, J. Phillips,
44, ... Wood, Esq.,
45, Lord Eardley,
46, Hon. E. Cust.

Window containing the Arms.

15. Mary Southall's portrayal of the window which offended Pugin.

Unfortunately, the precise nature of his generosity is now lost in the mists of time in much the same way that the modern fashion of naming new streets and institutions after local councillors will undoubtedly present future – and sometimes, indeed, today's – inhabitants with the riddle of *what* exactly they did to deserve the honour.

Edith Walk is an example of this type of riddle. Mary Southall described it as 'a charming promenade . . . extending from the grand entrance of the Library to the end of the village' but offered no explanation as to who or what Edith was. Possibly there is a connection with the Stoke Edith home of the Foley lords of the manor of Malvern.

A few members of the minor aristocracy had associations with Malvern and were acknowledged as benefactors. Such people were respected for their social status in a century where social class was of the utmost importance, reinforced by the teaching of the church. Mrs. Alexander's hymn, praising 'All things bright and beautiful', originally

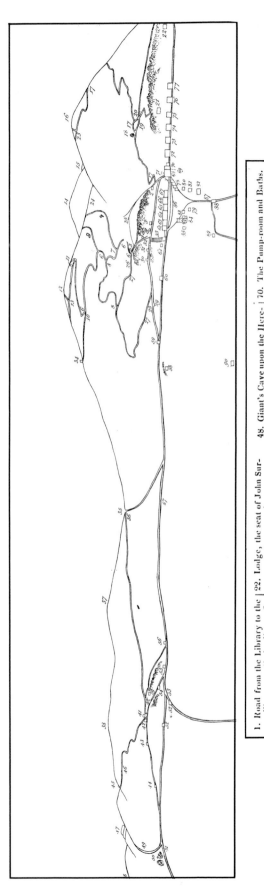

1. Road from the Library to the Zig-zag walk, leading to St. Ann's Well, and Worcestershire Beacon.
2. The Shrubbery Lodging-house.
3. Ash Grove, the residence of the late Rev. James Stillingfleet, prebendary of Worcester Cathedral.
4. Zig-zag walk.
5. St. Ann's Well.
6, 6, 6, 6. St. Ann's Walk to the Worcestershire Beacon.
7. Direction rock to the Sugarloaf and Table-hill.
8. Buchanan's walk.
9. Merrick's walk to the Sugarloaf.
10. Walk to Harcourt Tower.
11. Round the summit to the Worcestershire Beacon.
12. The Worcestershire Beacon.
13. To Harcourt Tower, from the Beacon.
14. Sugar-loaf Hill.
15. Table Hill.
16. North Hill.
17, 17. Lambert walk, from the foot of the Shrubbery House, extending to the top of the North Hill.
18. Ivy Rock.
19. Talbot walk, leading to the North Terrace.
20. A short walk down the hill.
21. Holly Mount, the seat of Thomas Woodyatt, esq.

22. Lodge, the seat of John Surman, esq. and temporary residence of the Dean of Worcester.
23. Grenville walk, round Table and Sugar-loaf Hills.
24. The valley separating the Worcestershire Beacon from the North Hill.
25. Seat upon St. Ann's Delight.
26. Knoil's Delight.
27, 27. Danter's Walk.
28. Foley Terrace.
29. Card's View.
30. Castle-house Lodging-house.
31. Hill-cottage Lodging-house.
32. Banister's-cottage Lodging-house.
33. Steps leading down to the village.
34. Harcourt Tower.
35. Wiche.
36. Harcourt walk.
37. Perseverance Hill.
38. The Pinnacle.
39. Miss Barry's Cottage.
40. Well-house, with public boarding-table.
41. Holywell.
42. Rockhouse Boarding-house.
43. Belmont Lodge.
44. South Lodge.
45. The Alcove, erected by the Lady Mary Countess Harcourt.
46. Walk to the Rockhouse.
47. Camphill, or Herefordshire Beacon.

48. Giant's Cave upon the Herefordshire side.
49. Road to Ledbury.
50. Little Malvern.
51. Road to Upton.
52. Mayplace.
52*. Gloucester House.
53. Principal road to Upton.
54. Essington's Hotel.
55. Ruby Cottage.
56. North Lodge.
57. Road from Hereford and Ledbury to Worcester.
58. The Firs Lodging-house.
59. Turnpike-house.
60. Melton-house, the residence of Dr. Bennet Garlike.
61. Parks, the seat of Miss West.
62. Mrs. Plumer's House.
63. Crown Hotel.
64. Belle Vue Hotel.
65. Miss Mason's Lodging-house, let in separate apartments.
66. Devereux Lodging-house.
67. Post-office Lodging-house, let in separate apartments.
68. Library Board and Lodging-house. Here a public Boarding-table is kept, for a select party, not exceeding fourteen persons.
69. St. Edith Lodging-house, let in separate apartments, or the whole house, as circumstances offer, with or without board.

70. The Pump-room and Baths.
71. Academy for young gentlemen.
72. Foley-arms Hotel.
73. Trafalgar Lodging-house.
74. Foley Lodging-house.
75. Laurel Villa.
76. Burford Lodging-house.
77. Colcough Place, two Lodging-houses.
78. Paradise-row.
1. Mr. Griffith's Lodging-house.
2. Ditto.
3. Mr. Waldron, Surgeon, Apothecary and Druggist. Here are apartments to let.
4. Mrs. Silvester's Lodging-house.
79. Sunday School house.
80. Viranda Cottage Lodging-house.
81. St. Ann's Cottage. Mr. Warren, Surgeon and Apothecary.
82. Livery stables.
83. The Vicar's House.
84. Church.
85. Abbey Boarding-house.
86. St. Edith walk.
87. Road to Bernard's Green.
88. Turnpike-house.
89. Chalybeate Spring.
90. School of Industry.

16. Mary Southall's map of the principal walks and landmarks on the hills.

INSCRIPTION	TRANSLATION
placed in an Alcove	of a Latin Inscription, placed in an Alcove upon the
ON	
THE MALVERN HILLS.	MALVERN HILLS.
	THE ALCOVE AND SEATS,
PERGVLA. AC. SEDIBVS	WHICH
QVAS.	THE NOBLE LADY
CLARISSIMA. DOMINA. MARIA COMITISSA.	MARY COUNTESS HARCOURT
HARCOVRT.	HAD ERECTED,
IN. VSVM. ORAMBVLANTIVM.	UPON THE SALUBRIOUS SUMMIT OF THESE DELIGHTFUL HILLS,
IN. SALVBERRIMO. VERTICE.	FOR THE ACCOMMODATION OF PERAMBULATORS,
HORVM. AMOENISSIMORVM. COLLIVM.	HAVING BEEN
EREXERAT.	DURING THE LAST WINTER,
HYEME. NOVISSIMA.	MALIGNANTLY DESTROYED BY FIRE;
MALIGNE. CONCREMATIS.	THE NEIGHBOURING INHABITANTS AND VISITORS
HAS.	OF THE SPOT,
VICINI. INCOLAE. FREQVENTATORESQVE. LOCI.	FEARING LEST THIS MARK OF SINGULAR BENEVOLENCE
NE. SINGVLARE. BENEFICIVM.	FROM THAT EXCELLENT LADY,
NOBILIS. FOEMINAE.	TO WHOSE
CVJVS.	CHARITY, LIBERALITY AND BENIGNITY,
PIETATEM. LIBERALITATEM. ET. BENIGNITATEM.	THE HIGHEST HILLS AND HUMBLEST VALLIES, EVERY WHERE
JVGA. MONTIVM. HVMILESQVE. VALLES.	AROUND,
CIRCVNQVAQVE. TESTANTVR.	BEAR AMPLE TESTIMONY,
MEMORIA. SENSIM. EXCIDERET.	SHOULD BY TIME BE EFFACED FROM MEMORY,
GRATO. ANIMO.	HAVE,
INSTAVR. ET. RESTIT.	WITH GRATEFUL FEELINGS,
C. C.	CAUSED THE SAME TO BE RESTORED,
MENSE. AVGVSTO.	IN THE MONTH OF AUGUST,
MDCCCXXI.	1821.

17. According to T. C. Turberville's chronicle of Worcestershire in the 19th century, the alcove in which this notice was placed was roofed with iron and was struck by lightning on 1 July 1826. Three sisters and a friend were killed, their brother and two other sisters being seriously injured, all of them being 'laid prostrate on the ground'. The Latin inscription does not seem entirely a good idea: it seems rather pompous and, human nature being much the same throughout the ages, may have made the vandals feel like repeating the damage which so incensed their social superiors.

contained a verse now familiar only to those who went to school in less egalitarian times than the second half of the 20th century:

> The rich man in his castle,
> The poor man at his gate;
> God made them high or lowly
> And ordered their estate.

Lady Spencer gave her name to a short walk below the Well House, Lady Harcourt to a tower on the slopes of the Worcestershire Beacon, as well as to several walks. Lady Mary, Countess of Harcourt, visited Malvern every year and paid for the cutting of 'many miles of road . . . from the Well House, round the hills, to St. Ann's Well, and round the beautiful Camp Hill'. She also financed the setting up of seats and shelters, the vandalism of which infuriated her contemporaries and reminds us that such anti-social behaviour is not peculiar to the modern age. 'To perpetrate their abhorrence of the act and to bear testimony to her ladyship's goodness, the inhabitants and visitors' placed an 'inscription' in an alcove on the hills.

The aristocratic name most used in Malvern today is that of Lyttelton. The Lyttelton Rooms in the priory churchyard and Lyttelton House near the Abbey Gateway derive their name from a lady described in 1819 by John Chambers as one 'who has for many years exerted herself, and continues to watch over the morals of the lower orders of

18a. This view of St Ann's Well, from the little known *Metropolis of the Water-Cure*, published in 1858, shows the original well-house before the Victorians added the mushroom-like stone building to the left. In the 1820s Mary Southall wrote 'A few paces from the well are conveniences for hot and cold bathing'.

18b. An early stereoscopic picture, again showing the original St Ann's well-house.

society round Malvern'. The poor woman had had some cause in her own life to reflect upon the morals of the higher orders of society, too, but was presumably powerless to do much on that score. Despite Chambers' typically 19th-century emphasis on class, Lady Lyttelton does indeed seem to have been a woman with her heart in the right place, her concern for others perhaps originating in her own experience of unhappiness. She did not lack the material comforts so obviously missing from many lives, but the thorough research of Brian Smith has exposed a life overshadowed by unhappiness. Born in 1743 into the Cotswold squirarchy of the Witts family, she set off in 1769 on the long journey to India where she was to marry a cousin devoted to her. By the time of her arrival this young man had died. She was overwhelmed with grief but recovered quickly enough to marry, in 1770, the rich governor of Calcutta, Colonel Peach. He, too, a victim of fever and the relentless Indian climate, died within six months and she returned to England a wealthy widow. Her money attracted the unscrupulous Thomas Lyttelton who wooed and won her in 1773. His behaviour led to their separation.

She settled in Malvern about 1800, staying here until her death in 1840. Her foundation of the building in the priory churchyard is well documented by both Mary Southall and John Chambers.

> When her ladyship married Colonel Peach, he presented her with a valuable set of filagree [*sic*] dressing-plate. She determined, at one time or other, to dedicate its value to some charitable purpose. She first intended to endow some houses for widows, but finding the state of the children about Malvern was miserable, from a total want of religious instruction, she resolved to honour the memory of the donor by laudably applying his gift to the erection of a Sunday school.

In 1814 she persuaded Edward Foley to grant the land and set up a body of trustees to ensure that the building should never be used for any other purpose than that of a Sunday school to cater for up to ninety children. Every September a sermon was to be preached in the priory church, the proceeds from the collection going to the Sunday school charity. During her lifetime Lady Lyttelton appointed the master and mistress of the school and, in addition, 'a necessitous widow or spinster' to live rent-free in the adjoining cottage, whose task was to keep the school house clean. Although the building has long since been altered to serve other needs specifically forbidden at the time of the foundation, the plans still make interesting reading:

> The long room, on the ground floor, is appropriated for the children to dine. Each child brings his dinner, whether living near or distant. This rule being a condition of admittance into the school, suitable tables are provided for them, with seats, in which their new garments are always locked up. This room Lady Lyttelton has ordered never to be converted into one for teaching. This part of the design includes in it, order, regularity and decency which are considered by the donor important and essential parts of education, and require to be strictly enjoined upon the lower orders of youth, of both sexes.

After this, the next comments seem curiously enlightened and modern:

> The committee exacts invariably from the master and mistress, mild behaviour to the children, and strict attention to the rules.

In addition to this school in the centre of the village, Lady Lyttelton set up another essentially 19th-century institution – a school of ancient industry – near her home at Poolbrook. This was sited next to her house, Peckham Grove, close to what is now the rear entrance to the Royal Signals and Radar Establishment. The contemporary description of this school again tells us a good deal about the class system then operating:

It being judged expedient that there should be instituted a school of real industry for poor females in the poorer classes of this parish, an unadorned building was erected near Peckham Grove, her lady-ship's cottage, in which is a room, 35 feet by 14, suitable for the work carried on by children, who are taught to card and spin wool, flax and hemp, knitting and every kind of common needlework; such as making and mending coarse garments, jackets and linen for the use of their parents and themselves. In this manner they may learn to produce their own garments of a cheap and substantial kind, suitable to their condition in life, as in former ages. In order to preserve to society, a useful hardy peasantry, it is intended to encourage field work; and that this employment may not be the means, as heretofore, of corrupting the morals of young persons, one of the matrons of the school always attends and works with them. Reading is regularly promoted; religious duties instilled, and industry is encouraged by an exact account being kept of their respective earnings. The lord of the manor, Edward Foley, Esq. generously gave some timber for the building of this school, and

19. The firm-set mouth and chin, offset by the open kindly eyes in this print of Lady Lyttelton, perhaps give a useful key to her character.

united with the Rev. Henry Card and the several land and free-holders, in granting leave to enclose some waste land for the school, and many of them assisted in the work by drawing materials to the spot; a pleasing proof of the unanimity and zeal for the benefit of the poor and highly creditable to the parish.

The school mistress was paid 16 shillings a month and money had to be raised to finish off the building and pay running costs. Just as today loyal supporters of charities hold coffee mornings and jumble sales to bring in cash, so Lady Lyttelton performed the genteel 19th-century equivalent:

Lady Lyttelton would be happy to see Lady W. and friends on Tuesday the 9th of October at eleven o'clock in the School of Industry, and afterwards, to take a sandwich in her new cottage on the Chase. Peckham Grove, 27th of Sep. 1821.

Such schools as these became redundant with the passing in 1870 of Forster's Act which laid the basis for nationwide elementary education financed by the state. In 1871 Lady Lyttelton's Sunday school became a boys' grammar school which eventually closed at the end of the Second World War and her School of Industry disappeared almost without trace. Lady Lyttelton's death in 1840 itself was a closing event in the history of old Malvern. In 1842 occurred an event which meant that the village would never be the same again.

Chapter Three

Malvern Becomes a Town

In 1842 Dr. Wilson and Dr. Gully, pioneers of the water-cure, arrived in Malvern, heralding 30 years of change that was to produce the spa town, with its new hotels and boarding houses, railway stations and all the other attractions of a community that earns its living from serving the public: in Malvern's case it was a genteel and respectable middle-class public.

In 1846 the remarkable Lady Emily Foley inherited her husband's estates and spent the rest of the century ruling Malvern with a firm matriarchal hand. By strange coincidence the same year, 1846, saw the breaking up and sale of one of the largest estates in Malvern – that of the Mason family. Building development was to be controlled by the ever-present hand of Lady Foley and the legal hand of the vendors of the Mason property – a formidable combination that could have taught even today's town planners a lesson or two.

These middle years of the 19th century saw the setting out of new roads with well proportioned detached and semi-detached houses in spacious gardens. Contracts required that purchasers should conform to numerous clauses and should:

> not . . . clean or scour or permit or suffer to be cleaned or scoured any horses carriages or vehicles of any description in the said roads

> nor permit or suffer any carpet or carpets to be cleansed or shaken in the said roads

> nor will allow any horse or horses to be exercised by Servants along the said roads

20. Lady Emily Foley in her youth.

> nor will place or deposit or allow to be placed or deposited any coals, ashes manure rubbish soil building materials or other goods in or upon the said roads . . . unless the same shall be immediately removed therefrom and not suffered to remain a longer time than is absolutely necessary for unloading and removing the same and that in case any ashes manure rubbish soil building materials

or other goods shall be brought to or carried from the said premises . . . the same shall be brought or carried away . . . before ten o'clock in the forenoon.

Purchasers were not to erect 'any row of houses or buildings other than single or double villas' nor any

messuage or tenement stable coachhouse pig stye or any other erection of any kind or description (except a boundary wall . . . contiguous to the before mentioned roads . . . and which said boundary wall . . . shall in no case exceed the height of five feet exclusive of any palisading to be placed thereon) within thirty-six feet of the said roads . . . nor within twenty feet of his boundary unless . . . he shall obtain the consent in writing of the proprietors of the adjoining land.

Nor were they allowed to build

any villa or residence or buildings connected therewith directly opposite to or in a parallel line with any other villa or residence so that the view from such last mentioned villa or residence shall be directly impeded or injured thereby.

Such clauses take up pages and pages of contracts of sale which form the earliest deeds of many of the buildings in central Malvern. This ensured high-class development to appeal to the rising middle-class, about a century before the state imposed building regulations.

The names of the new roads also have significance in our local or national history: Graham Road is a reminder that Lady Foley was born Lady Emily Graham, daughter of the Duke of Montrose, while Victoria and Albert Roads reflect a patriotic fervour that had but recently permitted the Queen's German consort such respect. Grange Road was the very heart of the Mason estate for it was at the Grange (next to the present Festival Theatre) that James Mason had lived until his death in 1846.

In 1851 the Great Malvern Improvement Act enabled 12 Commissioners to 'cause to be drained, cleansed, lighted, watched, regulated and otherwise improved the town of Great Malvern' using for the various purposes the General Improvement rate which they were empowered to levy at a level not exceeding two shillings in every pound of the full annual value of rated property. In addition they were allowed to levy a similar highway rate from time to time. Their work included the licensing and regulation of hackney carriages which then comprised any 'carriage drawn by any ass, mule, goat or other animal'. We learn, too, that drunken driving and possibly inappropriate punishments are not new phenomena peculiar to our modern way of life:

If the driver or person attending any such horse, mule, or ass, be intoxicated whilst driving or attending, or if any such driver, or other person, by wanton or furious driving, or by any other wilful misconduct, injure or endanger any person in his life, limbs or property, such driver or other person shall be liable to a penalty not exceeding five pounds.

Our modern separation of general rates from water and sewerage rates has its origin in the 19th century but when water rates began to be levied the supply for domestic purposes did 'not include a supply of water for baths, or for any manufacturing or hydropathic purposes, or for watering gardens or for fountains, or for any other ornamental or horticultural purposes'. One wonders what exactly it did include!

Gas came to Malvern in 1856, providing the first effective street lighting as well as a gradual extension of piped domestic supplies. The opening of the gas works was an occasion for great celebration, a bonfire being lit on the Worcestershire Beacon.

The first local newspaper was founded in 1855, at first being published only during the summer season, bidding its readers farewell in October until its return the following spring. Later on this *Malvern Advertiser* faced rivalry from the *Malvern News* – both now defunct and replaced by *The Malvern Gazette*.

About 40 years after Mary Southall published her description of Malvern, her successor at the Royal Library published a guide to the town which outlined the major changes to have occurred since her time. It is worth quoting at some length, both for the information contained and for its flavour of respectability:

The TOWN of Malvern strangely contrasts with that vulgar succession of streets, courts, alleys etc that are usually so denominated. In place of streets it has a succession of fashionable mansions – in place of courts and alleys it has villas, crescents and terraces, and though TOWN in fact, it is little like one in external aspect: it has few buildings consecutively joined together, and consists chiefly of separate and distinct residences. These – built generally in the most costly styles of architecture – are on all hands interspersed by pleasure gardens and shrubberies, made beautiful by all the ornamentation that art and nature can afford. The town extends itself over a large area, and whether viewed from the plain below or hill above, the effect is most picturesque.

Within the memory of some of its inhabitants, Malvern consisted of a single chain of houses, dotted along each side of the road that leads to and from Worcester and Ledbury. Till within a recent period it possessed not either its Graham, Victoria or Albert Roads, and the whole of the South Fields district was without road, house or inhabitant: only two houses existing beyond the Priory Gateway, one of which, situate near the church, was a farm-house with fold-yard round it. In the district of the South Fields the reader now will find some of Malvern's most elegant and important buildings. The 'Abbey Hotel', the private residences and hydropathic establishments of Dr. Gully, Dr. Wilson and Rayner, Dr. Marsden, Dr. Johnson, Dr. Stummes and Dr. Grindrod are in this neighbourhood. Here also are situate some of the most fashionable villa residences, in which accommodation of the best kind is afforded to visitors. The roads in this neighbourhood are good, and its general arrangements admirable. This part of Malvern is much sought because of its quietude and retirement.

The centre of the town contains the 'Post Office', the 'Foley Arms Hotel', the 'Belle Vue Hotel' and 'Graefenberg House' – one of the earliest of Malvern's buildings and celebrated as the residence in which the practice of hydropathy was commenced. At the end of Church Street, a little way down the hill, is a large commercial and family hotel, known as the 'Beauchamp Hotel'. On either side of the Graham Road charming houses have been built, and are still building, the views from which are of the most pleasing and extensive character. Following the road down the hill, we pass 'Portland Place' – two large ornamental blocks of building – 'The Priory', 'Abbotsmead', 'The Pleasaunce' etc. Advancing nearer the Railway Station, on both sides of the way, a series of fine buildings meet the eye. Passing 'Lawnside', and one or two other unique residences, we find ourselves at length looking up at a vast palatial pile of building, the 'Imperial Hotel'. This building belongs to a Hotel Company, limited; fabulous sums of money have been lavished thereon: it is well fitted up, and its general arrangements are said to be of a complete character.

Proceeding a little northward, we visit 'Lansdowne Crescent', recently built, principally composed of lodging-houses let to visitors. Crossing to the 'Albert Road', in the distance we see 'Malvern Link', the 'Malvern Link Hotel' and a train of villa residences scattered along the side of the road between Malvern Link and Malvern. Passing 'Ivy Lodge' and 'Parkfield', looking toward the centre of town, we get a fine view of the place, with the tower of the church rising majestically in the midst. From this point a view is obtained of 'Holly Mount', the house in which our present QUEEN resided on visiting Malvern in 1830; it is seen embosomed in the wood at the foot of the North Hill. We also see from thence the whole of that range of houses that look out so conspicuously upon the landscape from the 'upper' or 'Worcester Road'. 'Pomona House', 'Davenham Bank' and 'High Croft', here form prominent objects in the picture. Ascending the hill a little, we meet with that ordinary accompaniment of civilisation, the 'Court House' and 'Police Station', a massive brick building, in which the magisterial business of the town is transacted; and as if on purpose to point a moral, opposite thereto is 'Trinity Church', its spire pointing heavenwards: from thence North Malvern is seen; a neighbourhood chiefly made up of cottage residences; it has however its neat villas and terraces, and is frequented by visitors.

In nothing are there greater contrasts presented than in the styles of architecture prevalent in Malvern. It has been affirmed that no two houses are exactly alike. The fine old church seems

21a. H. W. Lamb kept the Royal Library in the middle of the 19th century. He published a number of prints of the growing town, this one showing his library to good effect. The buildings along Belle Vue Terrace have survived more or less intact, with major alterations being apparent only to their lower floors.

21b. Another Lamb print which, despite a good deal of artistic licence, is accurate in the prominence given to the priory church and in the impression of open fields in the lower part of the parish of Malvern. Through these fields were driven the railway line and roads such as Avenue Road in the 1860s. The large houses along the Worcester Road were well established by this time.

21c. This Lamb print again shows the priory church. Just below the church and running off to the left of the picture is a path which may well be Mill Lane, later renamed Clarence Road.

22. These three pictures are very rare, being taken from mid-19th-century stereoscopic photographs. They show:

a. The Post Office on the site now occupied by W. H. Smith. The premises were then occupied by Mr. Cross, who also ran a stationery shop and 'select library'.

b. The southern end of Belle Vue Terrace.

c. William Archer's new *Abbey Hotel* and the south side of the gateway to the medieval priory.

greatly to have impressed itself upon the architecture of the place; hence, Tudor, Elizabethan, and the various combinations of Gothic are most prominent. Here and there, however, Swiss, Italian, Corinthian and what is called Continental Gothic are seen, and occasionally all styles seem jumbled together in most grotesque confusion. This house is built with stone, that with brick – this plain, that stuccoed – this white, that red – this one smooth and genteel, that one altogether rugged and romantic; each house has however its distinctive characteristic, each differs as a rule from the other, and generally monopolises to itself its share of admiration and approval.

The nomenclature used for houses in Malvern, as in most places of the kind, might form a curious study. Poetic imaginings have given us 'Byron' and 'Shelley' Cottages; military musings have left us with 'Wellington', 'Raglan', and 'Anglesea' Houses, 'Walmer' Lodges, and 'Alma' and 'Como' Villas; 'Rosli' and 'Sardinia' Houses call travel to remembrance; and 'Knotsford' Lodges, 'Abbey' Terraces, 'Priorys' and 'Abbotsfields' awaken thoughts of Malvern in her conventual days.

Malvern's 'conventual days' had ended in the 16th century when Henry VIII dissolved all monastic establishments; its water-cure days in the 19th century were more obviously significant in its development. The well-to-do who came for the water-cure expected high standards of service and tasteful surroundings. Malvern provided what they wanted and some of them gave the town more than money in return. To such visitors we turn for accounts of life at the water-cure and for a contemporary view of some of the principles behind it.

Hydropathy . . . is in one word, sympathy . . . It is on this principle of sympathy . . . that all hydropathic treatment turns. What a beautiful text that is in our Scripture: 'If one member suffers, all the members suffer with it' How true it is, if you feel disease or debility, through the whole of the system, you may depend upon it that results from the instinctive sympathy of every part of the system, to save some one fatally affected part . . . Do you not see here a very important distinction between the system of Hydropathy, and the old medical system? The old medical system attacks the disease as it lodges in the villages and outworks of the system . . . Hydropathy attacks the metropolitan cities and central citadels . . . Dr. Gully, in his clever book on the 'Water-cure in Chronic Disease', likens the stomach, under the old system of treatment, to an amphitheatre in which combat is going on, not between disease and the medicine, but between a number of medicines which your druggist has put into your stomach, every one of which is striving to get the upper hand, while the disease which was really the object of thought is altogether forgotten in the combat.

(From *The Metropolis of the Water Cure* by *A Restored Invalid*)

23. Lane's sketch of the shallow bath.

The new answer to curing chronic disease was pure water, taken internally to wash out the system and applied externally to ensure relief to any malfunctioning parts. Patients came to Malvern for several weeks at a time, placing themselves in the care of a hydropathic doctor in his establishment or in one of the hotels or boarding-houses visited regularly by the doctors. The régime was strict, typically starting at 6 a.m. when the patient was awakened and 'packed'.

At six the bath attendant appeared with what seemed a coil of linen cable, and a gigantic can of water ... I was ordered out of bed and all the clothes taken off. Two blankets were then spread upon the mattress, and half over the pillow, and the wet sheet unfolded and placed upon them.

Having stretched my length upon it and lying on my back, the man quickly and most adroitly folded it – first on one side and then on the other, and closely round the neck, and the same with the two blankets, by which time I was *warm*, and sufficiently composed to ask how the sheet was prepared to the proper degree of dampness ... Two more doubled blankets were then put upon me, and each in turn tucked most carefully round the neck and under me. Upon this the down bed was placed, and over all another sheet or counterpane was secured at all sides and under the chin, to complete this hermetical sealing ... I was fast asleep in five minutes.

(From *Life at the Water Cure* by R. J. Lane)

An hour later the patient was extracted from the packing – an awakening to which he reluctantly submitted – and given a shallow bath, all too vividly portrayed in R. J. Lane's sketch. After a brisk rubbing down, a walk was taken to drink water fresh from the spring. St Ann's Well, being the nearest for most patients, was particularly popular and was described by 'A restored invalid':

I have just come from St. Ann's Well. I wish you had been up there with me at six o'clock this morning ... attended as I went by a number of travellers, some on donkeys ... to be sure, what a festive scene the old place presented. A band was playing, as it plays every morning. A number of persons were assembled around the well, sitting, standing or walking, but each and all occupied from time to time in drinking the water which trickles out of a marble mouth into a marble basin, in a romantic little room. The whole of the surrounding hills were alive with people. Far away, up to the heights of the Worcestershire Beacon ... the entire of the slopes ... were thronged with multitudes seeking health, where health is truly to be found – from cold water, mountain breeezes, and exercise.

Breakfast followed at about 9 a.m. and consisted typically of a variety of breads ('all in perfection'), milk for those allowed it and, of course, water. After breakfast, a consultation with the doctor might follow and could well result in orders for treatment even more startling than the wet sheet and shallow bath. One's first douche aroused some apprehension but Lane clearly enjoyed his:

I have had my experience of this glorious bath. Every symptom proves that it agrees with me. It was an anxious point with me to take it discreetly ... First on the back between the shoulders, then down the spine, then on the right shoulder, and on the whole of the right side; *never on the head* until, having received it one full minute, I placed my hands (the fingers interlaced) over my head, and so broke the compact column into a delicious shower of foam. The fall of water is nearly twenty feet from the cistern. A pipe descends about two feet from the cistern, tapering downwards to concentrate the force of the fall.

24. The douche.

H. MANNING,

GOLDSMITH AND WATCHMAKER.

Watches, Clocks, and Time Pieces, in great variety

Finished by English Workmen, and Warranted.

JEWELLERY OF THE NEWEST AND MOST FASHIONABLE DESIGNS,

IN

CHAINS	GOLD AND SILVER PENCIL	LOCKETS
BROOCHES	CASES	BROOCHES, FOR MINIA-
BRACELETS	CHATELAINS	TURES
NECKLACES	RINGS	SHAWL CHAINS & PINS.

ALSO A

Large Variety of Silver Brooches & Bracelets,

SILVER FISH SLICES, CAKE CARVERS, FRUIT KNIVES, MELON CARVERS, BUTTER KNIVES, PICKLE FORKS, &c., IN CASES.

GOLD AND SILVER-MOUNTED SCENT BOTTLES.

Vinegarettes and Card Cases, with Views of Malvern.

25. Holyrood Terrace, the row of buildings opposite the *Foley Arms*, was a prime shop site at the height of the water-cure. Mr. Manning doubtless did a good trade. Notice the fashion for a wide variety of silver serving utensils at a time when the middle and upper classes had servants to clean them.

26. These three mid-19th-century romanticised prints convey much of the atmosphere of the expanding village in which water and tranquillity were so vital.

a. Dr. Wilson's Priessnitz House, built in 1845. From its windows and balcony at first-floor level, patients had views across what is now Priory Park.

b. The ancient priory church itself dominates the scene here; in the foreground the pool is shown with some of the swans which gave it its name. To the right of this idyllic spot was the site chosen by Dr. Gully for his home, The Priory (now District Council property).

c. Malvern liked to attract well-to-do visitors such as these at the Chalybeate Spa. Dr. Wilson took offence at comments made by his old friend, Dr. Gully, in *The Water Cure in Chronic Disease*; in pique, having bought the Chalybeate Spa, he excluded Gully's patients from it.

Whilst Lane's experience was very happy, he tells of others which were less so:

> In a corner of one dressing room is a broken chair. What does it mean? A stout lady – being alarmed at the great fall from the cistern; to reduce the height – carefully placed what *was* a chair, and stood upon it. Down came the column of water – smash went the chair to bits – and down fell the poor lady prostrate. She was better after a week.
>
> The force of the water may be conceived from this fact. Last winter a man was being douched, when an icicle that had been formed in the night was dislodged by the first rush of water, and fell on his back. Bardon (the attendant) seeing the wound and the plentiful bleeding, stopped the Douche in alarm – but the Douchee *had not felt* the blow as any thing unusual. He had douched daily, and calculated upon such a force as he had experienced.

The main meal of the day was dinner, served by Dr. Wilson at 3 p.m. Food was plainly cooked, leg of mutton frequently making an appearance, accompanied by potatoes and green vegetables. Variety was offered in the shape of veal or fish and, on Sundays, the treat of roast beef. The main course was followed by a milk pudding, rhubarb tart or something equally wholesome but not rich.

Dr. Wilson was of the opinion that dinner should be followed by at least half an hour's rest, and he forbade even the writing of letters at this time: 'Nothing so surely sends the blood to the head and irritates the stomach.'

Free time during the morning or afternoon was spent by healthily walking or lazily driving through the picturesque roads and lanes around Malvern. Madresfield, seat of the Beauchamp family, was described by R. J. Lane as 'very romantic, abounding in a great variety of trees of magnificent growth'. He commented on the 'exquisite conservatories, the grapes in succession houses and pineries' as well as the carpets and tapestry inside the house. Trekking round stately homes is not apparently a very modern diversion for those with time on their hands.

After one such excursion Lane returned to take a sitz bath before supper, describing it as not disagreeable but very odd, a view endorsed by his accompanying sketch.

> For this bath it is not necessary to undress, the coat only being taken off, and the shirt gathered under the waistcoat, which is buttoned upon it; and when seated in the water, which rises to the waist, a blanket is drawn round and over the shoulders.

Supper at about 7 p.m. was followed by social conversation with other patients and an early bedtime was vital in order to cope with the next morning's exertions beginning at such an early hour.

As the success of Wilson and Gully became apparent, other doctors came to Malvern to set up similar establishments. The two pioneers themselves quarrelled but each achieved enviable reputations and material wealth.

The sitz bath described by Lane

Chapter Four

Victorian Heyday

By 1860 Malvern had certainly been shaken out of its rural seclusion and the next ten years saw two more major developments: the coming of the railway and the building of Malvern College.

The first passenger railway from Manchester to Liverpool had been opened in 1830 in an atmosphere of excitement mingled with fear as to whether the human body could withstand the extraordinary speed of 30 miles an hour. Despite many objections from those who were suspicious of such noisy modern monsters, railway mania gripped the nation and the countryside was covered with a network of lines in an astonishingly short space of time. By the late 1850s it was clear that Malvern would soon have its own station and eventually had no less than four. Two of them – Malvern Link and Great Malvern – were part of ambitious schemes, incorporating hotels, designed by the architect E. W. Elmslie. The *Link Hotel* later became a school, sadly demolished in the 1960s.

27. Elmslie's masterpiece the *Imperial Hotel*, designed to impress the affluent visitors to Great Malvern.

28. Elmslie's hotel, with its own approach to the platform at Malvern Link station, became a school after only a few years. The school was closed in the 1960s and the building was demolished. The site is now covered with modern residential accommodation overlooking the much altered Malvern Link station.

29. Malvern Link station earlier this century.

30. Two unusual early 20th-century views of Malvern College and its grounds.

At Great Malvern, we can still clearly see Elmslie's scheme, despite the inevitable 20th-century residential building and the disastrous fire which in 1986 gutted much of the station. Adjoining the station and linked to it by an underground tunnel was the grandest hotel in Worcestershire – the *Imperial*. Between the two a new road, originally known as 'The Avenue', was lined with lime trees while that part of it which bridged the railway line was graced with an elegant stone parapet on each side. In front of the station's main entrance were public gardens, illuminated at night by gas-lamps set upon massive stone pillars. Dr. Gully himself was much involved in this expensive undertaking and for some years was the chairman of the company which owned the *Imperial*. Although the *Imperial Hotel* was bought in 1919 by Malvern Girls' College which subsequently enlarged the building, Elmslie's grand design was not destroyed. Such a complex of buildings indicated that Malvern was at last well and truly on the map, attracting affluent visitors of the kind that the Foleys had long thought were suited to Malvern.

A number of developments culminated in the opening of Malvern College in 1865. The reputation that Malvern had acquired for its healthy environment, the ease with which it could now be reached on the train, the desire of local businessmen to cash in on these facts and the nation's growing awareness of the need for educational reform: all had their part to play in the founding at Malvern of one of the new breed of public schools. It was not easy: sport, one of the main activities in a public school, necessitated an early and costly levelling of what was the side of a hill, while the endowments of the older generation of public schools were not available in a school which was newly

31. Rather appropriately, Oxleys music-shop took over Malvern's first concert hall, Cecilia Hall, named after the patron saint of music.

a. The hall in Church Street was used for many years by Oxleys as a rather grand showroom for their pianos. In recent years it has been carefully restored and the threat of demolition which once hung over it has now gone.

b. Oxleys out on business.

32. The Assembly Rooms, opened in 1885. Considerably altered and modernised, they are still discernible in the Winter Gardens complex.

founded. But the problems were overcome and Malvern College has survived to become one of the success stories of that period of educational experiment.

The growing number of visitors who had to be entertained necessitated the provision of some kind of assembly hall for concerts, balls and the like. Some time in the 1850s Cecilia Hall had been built but was too small to accommodate the increasing number of visitors. It was supplemented in 1883 by the Royal Spa Concert Hall near the Wyche Cutting and eventually, in 1885, made quite redundant when the Assembly Rooms and Winter Gardens were opened. The modern complex of Winter Gardens, theatre and cinema developed from this late 19th-century scheme set in Priory Park: the buildings were completely refurbished in the late 1920s preparatory to the first Malvern Festival in 1929 and have undergone several modifications and refurbishment from time to time since then.

The Winter Gardens and Park are now, of course, owned by the District Council, as is the Council House overlooking the park. What is often not realised is that Priory Park was Dr. Gully's garden and that the Council House is on the site of his house, known as The Priory: the park takes its name from his home, though doubtless he hit upon that name because of its proximity to the Priory Church.

Dr. Gully left Malvern in 1872 after dominating local affairs for the best part of 30 years. His former partner, Dr. Wilson, with whom his relationship had been rather chequered, died in 1867 and his own departure and subsequent death in 1883 meant that Malvern had lost the two men who did most for the town's fortunes in the 19th century.

A selection of pictures and advertisements to show the wide variety of accommodation available to visitors in the early 20th century.

THE BELLE VUE HOTEL
MALVERN.

33. A rare picture of the *Belle Vue Hotel* showing the steep slope of the hillside behind it.

34. The *Tudor Hotel*, seen here from what we now term the back, was where Dr. Gully practised for 30 years, keeping his male and female patients apart: he considered it 'of very doubtful propriety to place male and female patients in the same establishment'.

Gold Hill Private Hotel,
AVENUE ROAD,
GREAT MALVERN.

TELEPHONE 91.   Telegrams: "GOLD HILL, MALVERN."

This High-class Private Hotel and Boarding Establishment has been greatly enlarged and thoroughly modernised, having had several new bedrooms and a beautiful lounge added.   It will now be found replete with every comfort and convenience for Visitors and Invalids.

SPECIAL CUISINE FOR INVALIDS.

ELECTRIC LIGHT. LIFT. HEATED THROUGHOUT.

Motor Garage within three minutes.   Central for Brine Baths.
          Badminton.   Tennis.   Croquet.   Golf.

ILLUSTRATED BOOKLET WITH LOCAL VIEWS
ON APPLICATION TO— **Mrs. BRAY HARTLAND.**

35. & 36. The *Gold Hill* and *Aldwyn Tower* have both become rest homes.

ALDWYN TOWER MALVERN

Highest Boarding House in Malvern.   600 ft. above sea level

The above First-class Private Hotel and Boarding House will be found a most desirable place of residence for Winter or Summer. It is sheltered by the North Hill from the cold winds in Winter and early Spring, and shaded in Summer by fine trees. Every home comfort.

It is situated within three minutes from the centre of Town. Near by is the Manor Park Croquet and Tennis Lawns.   Fifteen minutes from Golf Links. Wide Stone Balcony extends the whole length of the house, commanding exquisite views.

Terms, Tariff, etc., apply—
Mr. and Mrs. FRED J. SMITH

Malvern

MAY PLACE
A.A. AND R.A.C.
Residential Hotel,
MALVERN WELLS

GARAGE.   "GRISELDA" HARD TENNIS COURT.

Beautifully situated upon the slopes of Malvern Hills, 500 ft. above sea level. Commanding magnificent views across the Severn Valley. Roomy and comfortable.   —   Electric light. Water from the famous Holy Well laid on. Motor 'Buses from Malvern, Worcester and Birmingham pass the door.   G.W.R. and L.M.S. Stations near.

TARIFF FROM
L. CLENNELL, Proprietor.

'Phone or Wire: MALVERN 138.

Quite near New Golf Course.

37. A school was set up at May Place in 1856. It later became a hotel and then private residential accommodation.

38. Dr. Wilson's Priessnitz House was extended after his death. It later became the *County Hotel* and then, in the 1940s, a hostel for workers at the scientific establishments. In the 1980s it was refurbished and sold off to individuals as apartments.

39. The Misses Dowding at Trafalgar House, Great Malvern. The house, next to the *Foley Arms Hotel*, was divided into apartments.

Chapter Five

The End of an Era

On the national scene an era ended in 1901 with the death of the queen who had reigned since the age of 18 and had, after nearly 64 years on the throne, given her name to an age and appeared to many to be indestructible. Just one year earlier another matriarchal figure – Lady Emily Foley – had died. For Malvern, the death of its lady of the manor was the closing of an important chapter in its history and the fact that she had breathed her last on 1 January 1900, in the first hours of the 20th century, must have served to underline the sense of a new age dawning. Born in 1805, she was the fourth daughter of the Duke of Montrose and so enjoyed a higher status in society than the man she married in 1832, Edward Thomas Foley, some 14 years her senior. But he was no pauper and when he died childless in 1846 she took over his extensive estates and ruled them with skill for the next 54 years. Their home in Stoke Edith was destroyed by fire in the early 20th century but their archives may be studied in the Record Office in Hereford. On the wall of Stoke Edith church is an outsize commemorative plaque bearing an epitaph to this formidable couple. One suspects that Lady Foley may have chosen her own epitaph. Taken from the book of Nehemiah it reads: 'Think upon me, my God, for good, according to all that I have done for this people.' Like most of her class, Lady Foley was as aware of what was due to her quite as much as what was expected of her!

By the turn of the century Malvern's golden age seemed to be over. The water-cure no longer attracted visitors. The sceptics and an unfortunate episode of typhoid had put an end to hydropathy though there were still valiant – and fairly successful – attempts to sell Malvern as a health resort to young and old alike:

> Even to the less vigorous and to those advanced in years there need be no difficulty in seeing everything of interest in the vicinity . . . On the hills themselves are splendid roads . . . So well kept are they and so easy is their slope that motor-cars have safely reached the summit and returned.
>
> (from *Malvern: In and Near*)

The last sentence – with its triumphant final two words – is a remarkable tribute to the motor-car in its uncertain early days and by no means an invitation to the modern motorist who would be breaking the law if he sought to drive up the hill paths.

> Everything is scrupulously clean, as befits a health resort; there is nothing to offend the eye or other senses, no garish or gaudy decoration, the only touches of brilliant colour being the numerous flowers, whose well-being and luxuriance are a living testimony to the healthiness of the surroundings. The water is as pure as it is possible to obtain, and its source of supply and the surroundings of the storage reservoir rigidly guarded from any possible contamination. The fact that the Malvern death rate is the lowest annual one appearing in the Registrar General's return, among similar health resorts, is in itself the surest practical guarantee of the perfection of its hygienic conditions.

To this haven the 'splendid expresses' of the Great Western Railway could whisk the care-worn Londoner in a mere two and a half hours, a time that has not been significantly improved upon during the course of the 20th century. At the same time as commenting on the health and longevity of Malvern residents, the same guide-book advised:

> For the jaded in mind and body . . . a restful visit to our Malvern Hills acts in a wonderful manner. The vital forces are rapidly recuperated, and fresh energies quickly succeed listlessness and languor.

These peculiar bracing, tonic and invigorating effects of Malvern air . . . seem to be due to a variety of causes. To mention a few of the most obvious, there is (a) Comparative freedom from organic dust and germs, due to elevation and exposure to prevailing winds; (b) Entire absence from vitiation caused by town smoke and refuse, or the gaseous discharges of busy manufacturing centres; (c) Absolute immunity from the malarial exhalations of low-lying and marshy districts, where is much decaying vegetable and animal matter in the presence of water; (d) Dryness, being remote from lakes and rivers; and (e) Abundance of ozone, this being confirmed by repeated tests throughout the year.

Fresh air and opportunities for invigorating walks with the added advantage of beautiful views certainly continued to encourage visitors but another blot appeared on the landscape when the national demand for roads suitable for the new-fangled motor-car led to the Malvern Hills being quarried to provide stone. For about 30 years the future of Malvern seemed uncertain: was it to become a quarry town dominated by the noise, dirt and damage of daily blasting out of tons of stone or was it to retain its genteel image, earning its livelihood from providing services like education and holidays for the middle-classes?

By this time the taking of photographs and the sending of postcards had become very popular, so that our contemporary glimpses of Malvern become increasingly pictorial and include several pictures published by local shopkeepers whose businesses no longer exist. The provision of free education for every child at the end of the 19th century undoubtedly encouraged the postcard trend. In those far-off days of fast reliable mail services but scant telephone facilities people dashed off postcard messages in the way that we today use the telephone to organise our social and domestic life. 'I shall be down by the 5.50 tomorrow', 'Just to let you know I got back all right', or 'Will you kindly ask if they will take me half a loaf of bread, also some potatoes and ask the milkman to leave a quart of milk' are typical messages from postcards.

The spread of education encouraged the publication of guide-books, newspapers and journals but also seems to have coincided with a belief that readers cannot cope with more than a few very simple sentences at a sitting. The increased use of 'journalese' has robbed us of many pleasures, not the least of which is the supply of detailed information so beloved of the Victorian writer. Today we get our opinions prepacked, like our food, with a corresponding blandness. This makes it less worthwhile to quote from contemporary guidebooks and encourages the use of visual sources to illustrate Malvern's history.

Chapter Six

The Malverns in the Early 20th Century

For centuries several distinct communities had clustered round the Malvern Hills. These, like central Malvern, expanded in the 19th and early 20th centuries. The pictures which follow highlight some of the features, not only of Great Malvern, but also of these other centres of population which saw themselves as separate villages.

Great Malvern

40. For many visitors to Malvern their first view on alighting from the train was up Avenue Road towards the hills.

41. The entrance to the *Imperial Hotel*, now the main building of Malvern Girls' College. Although still easily recognisable, it has lost its iron railings, lamps and trees. A little further up Avenue Road was the spot where horse-drawn cabs waited to take passengers from the railway station. A cluster of these vehicles can be seen under street lamps which may seem picturesque but provided rather feeble light.

42. Swan Pool.

43. Behind the trees lining Avenue Road, garden plots close to the railway line showed a practical purpose rather different from the Victorian emphasis on prettifying everything.

44. Swan Pool in winter at the turn of the century.

45. A picture of Priory Park dating from the 1930s when music from the bandstand added to the magic of the pre-war festivals. Later dismantled and put in the park at the Link, the bandstand eventually returned to its rightful home in the 1980s.

46a. & b. In 1935 the Lanchester puppets added to the magic of festival time. Waldo Lanchester, who had helped to found the London Marionette Theatre, at first gave shows in a marquee at St Ann's Pottery, shown here, where his wife worked as a potter. In 1936 a permanent marionette theatre was established at Foley House, a few doors along from the *Foley Arms*. The work of the Lanchesters – her pottery as well as their puppets – became known throughout the country. Their popularity lasted during and after the Second World War.

47. An unusual view, about 1905, of Rosebank House and the public gardens beneath it. The house itself was bought for the town in 1918 by C. W. Dyson Perrins. To its shame, the town allowed the house to fall into such disrepair that it was demolished despite the valiant efforts of the Friends of Malvern Civic Society, founded at the time of the proposed demolition, some 30 years ago.

48. When the Post Office moved to the top of Church Street its entrance was originally on the corner: the present entrance was part of the 1930s' refurbishment.

49. This picture of Belle Vue Terrace clearly shows where the vicarage stood, facing Belle Vue Island.

50. An unusual view from the gardens of the *Mount Pleasant Hotel*.

51. & 52. Two views from the bottom of Church Street taken in the first decade of the 20th century. Sparkes, on the site now occupied by Woolworths, had a forge adjoining their ironmongery. Higher up, opposite Oxleys piano and music shop, was the Ladies' Work depot kept by Miss Oakley.

53. The traffic is different, but the scene below the Church Street traffic lights has not changed greatly.

54. The shop fronts are very different, but the post box is still near Great Malvern's central crossroads.

55. The top of Church Street showing on the left Gazebo House, occupied by Hunt's tobacconists and the Malvern branch of Thomas Bennett, the photographer, who also had studios in Worcester.

56. Fonthill College, kept at the end of the 19th century by the Misses Geater, now houses the Great Malvern Antiques Arcade.

57. Worcester Road was resurfaced about 1924: at the back of this picture of the road works are the dairy and the *White Horse Hotel*, each supplying vital beverages for the inhabitants of Malvern.

58. The vehicle on the left helped to attract attention to 'Trigg's Drives for today' – they included one to British Camp and another round the hills.

59. Opposite Trigg's advertisement was the Royal Library, kept in the early 20th century by Woods.

60. The *Unicorn Hotel* was also kept by the Trigg family.

61. & 62. Two views of the Abbey Gateway showing some of the effects of its 1891 restoration. Although the postcard above was posted in 1915, the photograph was taken before the top of the gateway was embellished with stonework which some contemporaries considered to be so inappropriate as to amount to vandalism. The more recent picture, below, shows the shops adapted from the buildings which had formed the *Crown Hotel*'s stables, criticised as 'a disgrace to this charming village' in the early 19th century.

63. Malvern Priory Church, complete with its railings. The loss of so many railings is particularly sad now that we realise that their real contribution to the war effort was much less than was supposed at the time.

64. The front of Malvern College: the creeper on the walls made the building appear older than it actually was. A more practical modern age has removed it.

Malvern Link

65. & 66. Two views of the road just below Malvern Link station.

67. & 68. The lower end of Malvern Link Common has changed very little since these pictures were taken in the early 20th century.

69. When sold by the Foley estate in 1910, the Hermitage on Link Common 'would convert into a charming week-end cottage for a Birmingham businessman, as it is within a few minutes walk from Malvern Link Railway Station'.

70. The Colston buildings about 1905: there is still a chemist's shop on the corner, owned now by Brenda and John Guise. Other shops have been much altered, and the modern fronts have destroyed the original unity of the block. In 1915, No.7 was 'Maison Belge', inhabited by Belgian refugees who had fled the German invasion.

71. & 72.   The junction of Richmond and Worcester Roads.

Malvern Link, The Cross Roads

73.   For many years the premises at this junction were occupied by the Pembridge family of outfitters. Later, the
Midland Red bus office took over the site.

74. Just below
Pembridge's was the old-
fashioned tobacconist's
shop kept by Frederick
Fillmore.

75. Some of Fillmore's
customers pause for a chat
near the shop in the
Worcester Road.

76. Another view of the Worcester Road in about 1922.

77. These greenhouses stood at the junction of Spring Lane with the Worcester Road. A very different view now faces customers driving out of the Kwik Save car park!

The Santler car, driven by a steam engine and first tested on the Madresfield estate with the permission of Lord Beauchamp, was the first car to be produced in Malvern. The Santler family had set up business in Malvern Link in 1875 and earned their bread and butter by making and selling cycles during the late 19th-century heyday of the bicycle and tricycle.

Two brothers, Charlie and Walter Santler, experimented with various methods of propelling a small car, eventually rejecting the steam engine and a gas engine in favour of a petrol engine. By 1894 they were achieving speeds of 12 miles an hour – three times the legal maximum on the open road! The Santler brothers began to produce cars for sale until the early 1920s and the history of their first experimental vehicle has been something of a detective story unravelled by the vehicle's present owner, Dr. Alan Sutton. Sadly, the Santlers ceased production about 1922, having incurred heavy expense in developing a mechanised plough. The economic problems of the post-First World War period also adversely affected their fortunes as they did those of many large and small businesses throughout the world.

78.   The Santlers' experimental car, restored by Dr. Sutton.

79.   Malvern Link: on the right hand side of the road (in the middle of the picture) is a sign advertising Santler's garage.

Malvern Wells

80. & 81. It was the Holy Well which first attracted attention to the properties of Malvern water. For many years J. H. Cuff and Co. bottled the water but eventually the buildings became dilapidated. They were lovingly restored in the 1970s by Mr. John Parkes and officially re-opened in 1977, the event coinciding with the Silver Jubilee of Queen Elizabeth II. These photographs date from the early 20th century.

82. In the 18th and early 19th centuries many visitors stayed at the Wells House kept for years by William Steers. The old hotel is now a preparatory school, shown here about 1908.

83. Near the Holy Well the Rock House provided facilities for visitors who wished 'to live in a private manner' in the early 19th century. The restored house is now privately owned and occupied by residents who doubtless hope that present-day visitors will respect their privacy too!

Malvern Wells. Road to Holywell.

84. This picture shows that there was little difference in the quality of the road to the Holy Well and the main Malvern to Ledbury road. The latter has now become a temptation for speeding motorists, although long stretches of it are still lit by the old Victorian lamps.

85. Another view of the Wells Road, complete with historic street-lamp!

86. & 87. Two views of the junction at which stands St Peter's church, built in 1836 when Malvern Wells was still part of the large parish of Hanley Castle.

88. The Wells Road.

89. Few now notice the war memorial hidden by the hedges that have grown around it on the Wells Road. It was erected, like so many others, in a mood of sadness mingled with pride in the shocked but optimistic years before fascism reared its head in Europe. On the hill above may be seen the Wells House School, the former hotel kept by William Steers in the 19th century.

90. & 91.   Malvern Wells no longer has a railway station. In pre-nationalisation days it had two: one for the Great Western and one for the Midland line.

Little Malvern

92. Little Malvern priory church, remnant of the tiny medieval priory, looked like this in the early 20th century. Partial demolition when the monasteries were dissolved in the 16th century was followed by vandalism by parliamentarians in the 17th-century civil wars. A pathetic plea by the churchwardens in 1662 stated that the church was 'out of repaire' because 'of the late warrs' and it was impossible for the parishioners to repair the damage, 'it being known to be a very small poore place'. The misericord seats were hacked away, amongst other outrages. Nevertheless, the fragment of the priory that remained is now kept in good order.

93. & 94. Two idyllic views views before the motor car made it unwise to stand and stare in the middle of the road! The toll-house (*below*), built in the 18th century for the Upton Trust, has disappeared, but is safely preserved at the Avoncroft Museum of Buildings near Bromsgrove.

95. In 1915 the pass through the hills at the British Camp had not become a major tourist attraction, though some visitors stopped here and even surveyed the scene from the middle of the road where Herefordshire and Worcestershire met. Nearly 80 years later most of the land shown in the lower part of the picture is under tarmac and used as a main road and a car park. The two ancient counties are administratively, if not happily, united.

Barnard's Green and Poolbrook

96. & 97.   Already a small shopping centre in the early years of the 20th century, Barnard's Green has become much more built up in recent years. The thought of children playing on the island would today alarm us as we face the cut and thrust of driving round it – or simply stepping off to cross the road!

98. Although dating from about 1914, this picture is instantly recognisable as Barnard's Green.

99. & 100. W. H. Squibb established a grocery and provisions shop in the 1880s. He became renowned for his flour, with its 'lightness and digestibility' which appealed 'most powerfully to the palate of martyrs to indigestion'. His high reputation enabled him to move to larger premises.

101. Another local concern was that of A. E. Baylis who had two shops, one in Barnard's Green and the other in Church Street, Great Malvern. To this day, the chemist below the traffic lights in town bears the Baylis name, but the Barnard's Green branch, shown here, is recognisable only if you know where to look! This picture was one of many taken by C. D. Walton of Court Road (near the modern medical centre).

102. Gerald Ferris kept the tobacconist, sweet and newspaper shop at Bradford House in Barnard's Green. He published many pictures and this is his bird's eye view of Court Road.

103. The *Fountain Inn*, Court Road.

104.   Another view of Court Road, about 1923.

105.   About 1927 Mr. Kent came for a week and offered the excitement of a five-minute flight for five shillings. Flights took off from what was a field but now is part of the R.S.R.E. south site. Some time later Kent was killed in a crash.

106. Lydes Farm House, on the corner of Barnard's Green Road and the Pickersleigh Road, was rented out in 1910 for £22 a year! The agent did, however, admit that 'a small sum' was needed to bring it up to 'modern requirements'!

107. Moat Court Farm House, shown here in 1910, still enjoys a delightful position, despite extensive modern building.

108. Hastings Pool with, in the background, Barnard's Green House, home of Sir Charles Hastings, founder of the B.M.A. He was also consulting physician for the dispensary founded in 1830 to help the poor and infirm in Malvern.

109. An evocative view of Poolbrook.

110. The Mill Farm, close to Barnard's Green, was occupied in 1910 by Tilt Bros. It was the centre of a valuable estate which included six cottages and nearly 300 acres of 'undulating' land 'from which most beautiful views of Malvern and the Hills are obtainable'.

111. The Elms, one of several properties in the Guarlford Road sold by the Foley estate in 1910.

Link Top and North Malvern

112. Relics of ancient punishments as pictured at the turn of the century. They may still be seen at the bottom of Lodge Drive, off the North Malvern Road.

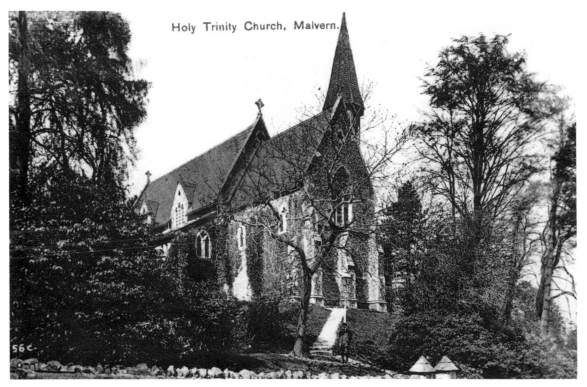

Holy Trinity Church, Malvern.

113. Holy Trinity church was built in the mid-19th century on a bleak and exposed site. Judicious planting provided this picturesque setting half a century later.

114. Trinity Hall looking very bright and new in the early years of this century, when the traffic was considerably lighter than it is today.

115. At the bottom of Bank Street William Bushnell kept his Link Top photographic studio.

116. The view from rooms near Bushnell's studio, rented by a visitor in 1913.

117. Newtown Road, Malvern.

Malvern Link Common.

118. Link Top at the start of the century, still recognisable today.

119. Just below the junction at Link Top was the house and shop of jeweller John Charles Moulder. Facing the common, it now houses the Eversley Stores.

120. Commercial quarrying took place in North Malvern for over half a century. It threatened the skyline of the hills, caused noise, damage and some danger – but also provided work for men in the period of high unemployment between the wars. This unusual picture shows not only the familiar tower which marks the old water tank in the North Malvern Road, but also the unsightly mess always associated with quarrying.

121. This view of North Malvern from the hills was taken in about 1910 before quarrying really took hold.

122. Despite the quarrying, there were still attractive views to be enjoyed at the northern end of the hills in 1917.

123.   At the junction of Cowleigh and North Malvern Roads stands Scotland House, now occupied by a car retailer. Some 70 years ago it was a drapers and outfitters. The upstairs windows are still the same.

124. Clarendon School in the Cowleigh Road was one of Malvern's many private schools, serving two or three generations of schoolgirls. After its closure as a school it fell into decay, but in 1988 the building arose again like a phoenix and was officially opened in January 1989 as council-owned accommodation for single persons in 25 apartments. Great care was taken to preserve features from the original building: the Victorian windows were salvaged, and attention to Victorian detail is apparent wherever one looks.

The Hills and West Malvern

125.   Jubilee Drive, about 1911: the drive was made to commemorate Queen Victoria's Golden Jubilee in 1887. Many locals objected to it because it used valuable common land and they regarded it as pandering to visitors.

126.   Going to the top of the Worcestershire Beacon: the toposcope was erected in commemoration of Queen Victoria's Diamond Jubilee. Donkeys were used on the hills for generations. This view is one taken by John Tilley of Ledbury, to whom all lovers of our heritage owe a tremendous debt. He tirelessly photographed street scenes, views from the hills and many aspects of everyday life until his death in 1924.

127 & 128. Two postcards of the Wyche: the message on the back of the card reproduced below includes the observation that 'a lot of soldiers have just gone past on horseback'. The card was posted in 1917, when the nations of Europe were war weary after devastating losses.

129.   Another turn of the century view of the Wyche Cutting.

130.   The road to St Ann's Well, *c*.1915, giving some idea of the effort required to walk to the well.

Road to St Anns Well.

131.   On the way to St Ann's Well.

132.   St Ann's Well became particularly
popular from the mid-19th century. For many
years until the 1930s blind George Pullen
played at the well. One of his instruments, the
Dulcitone, may be seen in Malvern Museum.
'Blind George' was also the organist at Storridge
church. Possibly he met Elgar there: when
Elgar rented a summer home at Birchwood he
frequently went to Storridge church.

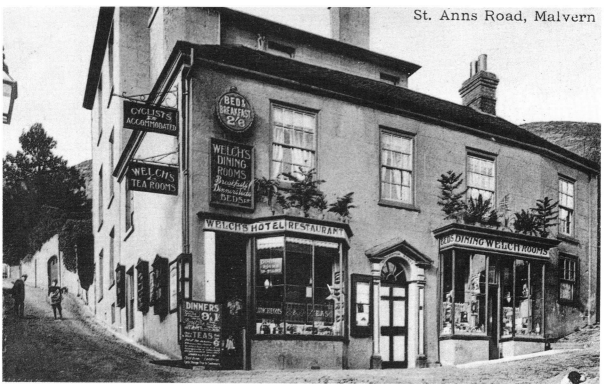

133.   Park Road, West Malvern.

134.   Croft Bank, West Malvern.

135.   The Meet, West Malvern.

136. & 137. Two views of the area around Malvern in the early 20th century provide food for thought. The harshness of the then new buildings is a healthy reminder that the modern yearning for an idyllic past is an indulgence in a myth.

Chapter Seven

Conclusion

Ultimately neither quarrying nor gentility won the battle for Malvern. The quarrying ceased due to changing commercial interests and a growing awareness of the fragility of our national heritage. After the Second World War one of the numerous Areas of Outstanding Natural Beauty designated by the government was centred on Malvern. As for gentility, such pretensions received short shrift during the war and Malvern was brought sharply into the modern age by the arrival in 1942 of the Telecommunications Research Establishment.The boys and staff of Malvern College moved temporarily to Harrow and scientists whose work was so vital to Allied success in the Second World War took over their buildings. To the displeasure of local residents, the scientists showed no signs of moving when the war ended in 1945. In 1946 they vacated the College buildings, but did not leave the town. The Royal Signals and Radar Establishment is today the biggest employer in the town and its closure would, therefore, now be seen by most locals as a major economic calamity for the area.

This is an excellent example of history's unexpected developments: a speculative venture into education by local businessmen in the 1860s led not simply to Malvern establishing a reputation in the educational world, but also to furnishing the town with the means by which many of its residents were to earn their living over a century later. No-one could have foreseen the long-term effects of that 19th-century business venture.

The continued viability of Malvern as a town is as much due to the existence of the Royal Signals and Radar Establishment as the transformation of Malvern in the 19th century was due to the water-cure. The scientists, at first so bitterly resented, injected a large measure of common sense and practical skills into the town and, once firmly ensconced here, the Establishment, which has undergone several changes of name and government policy, has remained consistent in one vital respect: it has attracted a workforce of highly articulate men and women who have insisted in a variety of ways, including the ballot-box, on the provision of good services in the area. It is not simply a matter of good fortune that local state schools, for example, maintain such high standards of work and behaviour – Malvern parents would soon make their views known if it were not so. Train services, library, theatre and other facilities are all of a much higher standard than might be expected in a town of some 30,000 people: locals often smile quietly to themselves when somewhat patronising visitors express surprise that a place so far removed from the so-called civilisation of a large town should have so much to offer, even to such cultured specimens as themselves. What Malvern has is quite unusual: it is not simply the economic power of the high percentage of its population in employment, with resultant good housing and other material benefits. Malvern is a town of doers rather than passive onlookers. This has ensured its survival and will surely continue to do so.

Malvern now attracts thousands of visitors each year and tourism is an important economic consideration. Many of these visitors do not venture into the town, their primary aim being to enjoy the freedom and fresh air of the hills. Those who do come into the town may, like so many locals, observe how attractive it is. Most of Victorian Malvern is still here for us to appreciate: the varied architecture, the Malvern stone houses and the lay-out of the main roads. Among both locals and visitors there is a strong desire, whilst enjoying many of the conveniences of modern living, to retain much of what the Victorians created. But perhaps the most valuable – and the most fragile – quality of Malvern is its provision of what a Victorian would have described as 'refreshment of mind and body'.

Bibliography

Card, Rev. Henry, *Dissertation on the Herefordshire Beacon*, 1822
Card, Rev. Henry, *Antiquities of the Priory of Great Malvern*, 1834
Chambers, John, *A General History of Malvern*, 1817
Fisher, Douglas, *Wooden Stars*, 1947
Foley Estate, *Sale Catalogue*, 1910
Grindrod, R. B., *Malvern Past and Present*, 1865
Gully, J. M., *The Water Cure in Chronic Disease*, 1859
Hurle, Pamela, *The Malvern Hills*, 1984
Hurle, Pamela and Winsor, John, *Portrait of Malvern*, 1985
A Restored Invalid, *Metropolis of the Water Cure*, 1858
Lamb, H. W., *Visitors Guide to Malvern*, c.1862
Lane, R. J., *Life at the Water Cure*, 1846
Lees, Edwin, *The Forest and Chace of Malvern*, 1877
Lines, H. H., *The Ancient Camps on the Malvern Hills*, c.1869
Malvern Development Assoc., *Malvern*, c.1930
Nott, James, *Church and Monastery of 'Moche Malverne'*, 1885
Oxley, A. C., *The House of Oxley*, c.1920
Smith, Brian S., *A History of Malvern*, 1964 and 1978
Southall, Mary, *Description of Malvern*, 1822
Stanford, S. C., *The Malvern Hill Forts*, 1973
H.M.S.O., *Great Malvern Improvement Act*, 1851
Stevens, M. T., *Malvern: In and Near*, c.1915
Sutton, R. A., *Malvernia: The First Santler Motor Car*, 1987
Turberville, T. C., *19th century Worcestershire*, 1852

Property deeds, prints, photographs and postcards

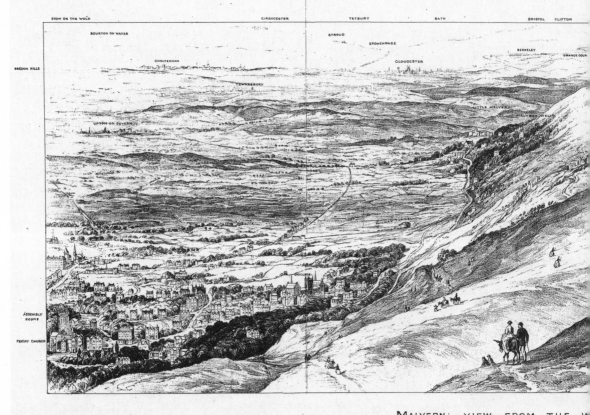

STOW ON THE WOLD   CIRENCESTER   TETBURY   BATH   BRISTOL   CLIFTON

BOURTON ON WATER   STROUD   STONEHOUSE   BERKELEY   GRANGE COUR

BREDON HILLS   CHELTENHAM   GLOUCESTER

TEWKESBURY   LITTLE MALVERN

UPTON ON SEVERN   MALVERN WELLS

BRANSLEY COURT

RAILWAY TUNNEL

ASSEMBLY ROOMS   COLLEGE

PRIORY CHURCH

MALVERN: — VIEW FROM THE W

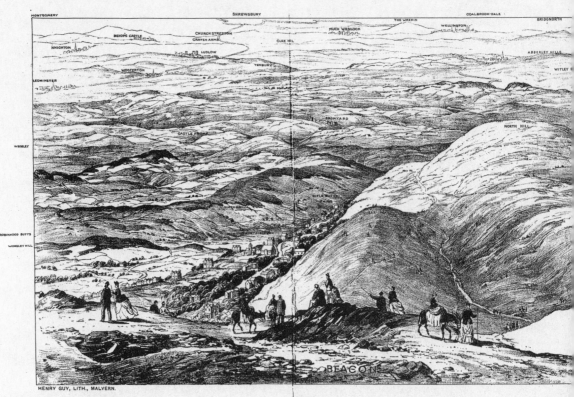

MONTGOMERY   SHREWSBURY   THE WREKIN   COALBROOK-DALE   BRIDGNORTH

MUCH WENLOCK   WELLINGTON

BISHOPS CASTLE   CHURCH STRETTON   ABBERLEY HILLS

KNIGHTON   CRAVEN ARMS   CLEE HILL

LUDLOW   WITLEY

WOOFFERTON   TENBURY

LEOMINSTER

BROMYARD

NORTH HILL

CASTLE FROME

WEOBLEY

ROBINHOOD BUTTS

WORSLEY HILL

BEACON

HENRY GUY, LITH., MALVERN.

MALVERN: — VIEW FROM THE